BUGGED OUT!
The World's Most Dangerous Bugs

TERRIFYING
TICKS

by Kevin Blake

Consultant: Paula L. Marcet, PhD
Research Biologist
Atlanta, Georgia

BEARPORT
PUBLISHING

New York, New York

Credits

Cover, © Westend6l Gm6H/Alamy; TOC, © KPixMining/Shutterstock; 4L, © Jane Ashley; 4R, © Goldyrocks/ Alamy; 5, © CDC/Science Source; 6L, © Jane Ashley; 6R, © CDC/Science Source; 7L, © Grambo Photography/ AGE Fotostock; 7R, © MeePoohyaphoto/iStock; 8L, © Juniors Bildarchiv GmbH/Alamy; 8R, © faustasyan/ Shutterstock, © Yoko Design/Shutterstock, © Jne Valokuvaus/Shutterstock, and © Astrid Gast/Shutterstock; 9, © Eerik/iStock; 10, © Juan Aunion/Shutterstock; 11, © Viscorp/Dreamstime; 12L, © Bernardo Pérez/ El Pais/Newscom; 12R, © StevenEllingson/iStock; 13, © anakopa/iStock; 14, © royaltystockphoto.com/ Shutterstock; 16L, © Grigorita Ko/Shutterstock; 16R, © nechaec-kon/iStock; 17, © Chutima Chaochaiya/ Shutterstock; 18L, © Laura Stirling; 18R, © Backyard Production/iStock; 19, © Science History Images/Alamy; 20, © rck_953/Shutterstock; 21T, © nechaev-kon/iStock; 21B, © thatreec/Shutterstock; 22 (T to B), © CDC/ Steve Glenn, © Melinda Fawver/Shutterstock, and © Falk Kienas/Alamy.

Publisher: Kenn Goin
Senior Editor: Joyce Tavolacci
Creative Director: Spencer Brinker
Photo Researcher: Thomas Persano

Library of Congress Cataloging-in-Publication Data

Names: Blake, Kevin, 1978– author.
Title: Terrifying ticks / by Kevin Blake.
Description: New York, New York : Bearport Publishing, [2019] | Series:
    Bugged out! the world's most dangerous bugs |
    Includes bibliographical references and index.
Identifiers: LCCN 2018047326 (print) | LCCN 2018048350 (ebook) |
    ISBN 9781642802375 (ebook) | ISBN 9781642801682 (library)
Subjects: LCSH: Ticks as carriers of disease—Juvenile literature. |
    Ticks—Juvenile literature.
Classification: LCC RA641.T5 (ebook) | LCC RA641.T5 B53 2019 (print) |
    DDC 571.9/86—dc23
LC record available at https://lccn.loc.gov/2018047326

For more information, write to Bearport Publishing Company, Inc., 45 West 21st Street, Suite 3B, New York, New York 10010. Printed in the United States of America.

10 9 8 7 6 5 4 3 2

Contents

A Black Speck

On a cool April morning in 2015, Jane Ashley started off on a hike near her Virginia home. With her dog Daisy by her side, Jane walked through fields of tall golden grass. The next day, Jane's daughter, Emma, spotted a black speck on her mom's back. Looking closer, Emma noticed that it wasn't a spot at all, but a tiny creature with eight legs. It was a tick! Emma quickly yanked it off.

Jane Ashley

Ticks often live in tall grass or on bushes or shrubs. They can also be found in lawns and gardens.

Days later, Jane began feeling very sick. She had developed a rash, felt achy all over, and experienced stabbing pain behind her eyes. Jane's pounding headache soon turned into a high fever. When she felt so ill she was unable to get out of bed, Jane decided to check herself into the hospital. What was making her so horribly sick?

Ticks are **arachnids**, like spiders and scorpions. They have eight short legs and oval-shaped bodies.

From a distance, a tick can look like a dark speck or a poppy seed. Ticks can often be found on very soft parts of a person's body, such as the armpits and inner thighs.

Mystery Illness

When Jane was in the hospital, her condition quickly grew worse. Her lungs filled with fluid, which made breathing difficult. Other **organs** also began to fail. Jane grew sicker by the hour. Because of the tick bite and rash, one doctor **suspected** that Jane had come down with Rocky Mountain spotted fever (RMSF). This deadly disease is spread by ticks. Luckily for Jane, he was right.

Jane in the hospital

RMSF often causes a rash, along with a fever, headache, and stomachache.

The doctor treated Jane with **antibiotics**. Slowly, she began to recover. Within a couple of weeks, Jane was back on her feet, though she was still feeling weak. As Jane left the hospital, she was tired but very grateful for, "the medical folks who helped me survive my illness." Now, Jane walks her dog Daisy in the park—and always checks herself and her pet for ticks afterward.

American dog tick

RMSF is often **transmitted** by the American dog tick, which is found mostly in the southeastern United States. RMSF is the most common **fatal** tick-**borne** disease in the country, causing about 15 deaths a year.

Certain kinds of ticks prefer to feed on certain kinds of animals. The American dog tick, for example, likes to prey on dogs.

Bloodsuckers

The American dog tick is just one of hundreds of kinds of ticks, some of which spread diseases. A tick is an **external parasite** that feeds on blood. To survive, the tick must first find a **host** animal to feed on. This tiny bloodsucker doesn't jump or have wings to fly. Instead, it perches on the end of a blade of grass or other plant and waits for an unsuspecting creature to walk by.

A tick waits for a meal on a blade of grass. It uses some of its legs to hold onto the grass. It will use its other legs to climb onto a passing animal.

Ticks have four basic life stages: egg, larva, nymph, and adult. Some species take up to three years to complete their life cycle.

Adult female

Adult male

Nymph

Egg

Larva

Once it finds a body to invade, the tick pierces its victim's skin with sword-like mouthparts. Then it inserts a feeding tube, which is similar to a straw, into the host and drinks its blood. Many ticks carry **bacteria**, **viruses**, or parasites in their **saliva**. When the tick bites, the infected saliva gets released into the host's blood. This can sicken the host and cause serious illnesses—some of which are deadly.

A blood-filled tick

Once attached to a host, the tick often feeds on blood for two or three days. A female tick can grow up to 100 times her original size after an especially large meal!

A Hairy Problem

Ticks can sicken people in many different ways, as five-year-old Kailyn Griffin of Mississippi and her mother found out. One morning, little Kailyn was trying to get dressed for school when her legs gave way. The child **collapsed** in a heap on the floor.

Like this child, five-year-old Kailyn Griffin was unable to walk.

Kailyn's mother ran into her daughter's room. As she helped her child up, she noticed a blood-filled tick attached to Kailyn's scalp. Alarmed, the mother plucked the tick off and rushed her daughter to the hospital. At the hospital, the doctors **diagnosed** Kailyn as having tick **paralysis**—a condition that causes numbness of the legs. Thankfully, Kailyn quickly recovered and was running and playing by the end of the day. "Check your kid for ticks," her mom warned other parents after the scary experience.

The tick in Kailyn's hair had likely been there for five to seven days before it was discovered. That's how long it usually takes for tick paralysis to set in.

Female ticks that are about to lay eggs produce a dangerous **neurotoxin** in their saliva. As a tick fills up with blood, it transmits the neurotoxin into its host. This is what happened to Kailyn.

Lyme Disease

Tick paralysis is very **rare**. Lyme disease, which is also transmitted by ticks, is much more common. In the summer of 1999, writer Amy Tan attended an outdoor wedding in upstate New York. Little did Amy know that before she returned home to California, a bloodsucking deer tick had attached itself to her body.

Writer Amy Tan wrote a best-selling book called *The Joy Luck Club*.

Deer ticks often prey on mice, deer, and other mammals and are responsible for spreading Lyme disease. Lyme disease is the most common tick-borne illness in the United States.

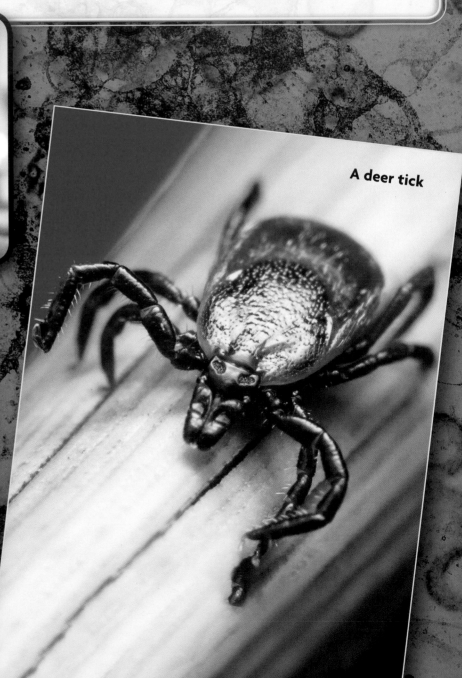

A deer tick

At first, all Amy noticed was a rash on her leg. After a month, red splotches covered Amy's arms. Other symptoms followed, including "a stiff neck, **insomnia**, a constant headache, and a bad back," according to Amy. After that, her health got even worse.

Lyme disease is named after the small town of Old Lyme, Connecticut, where the disease was first discovered in the 1970s. Each year, there are roughly 300,000 new cases of Lyme disease in the United States.

A red circular rash can be the first sign of Lyme disease. However, some people infected with Lyme disease never develop this rash.

Brain Attack!

Over time, the bacteria from Amy's tick bite spread to her brain, resulting in **lesions**. The brain lesions caused Amy to **hallucinate**. She was very scared. Not long after, Amy had trouble remembering. "I could not read a paragraph and recall what it said," she would later report. Other times, Amy felt as if she were in a fog. She was desperate to find out what was wrong.

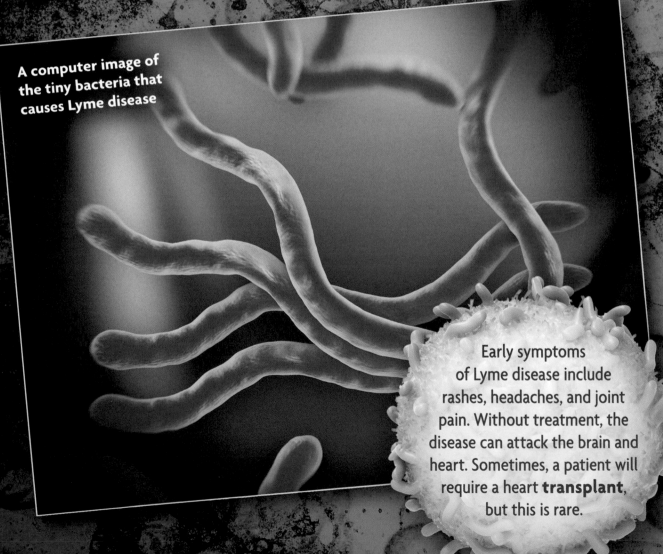

A computer image of the tiny bacteria that causes Lyme disease

Early symptoms of Lyme disease include rashes, headaches, and joint pain. Without treatment, the disease can attack the brain and heart. Sometimes, a patient will require a heart **transplant**, but this is rare.

After months of seeing different doctors and undergoing countless tests, Amy learned from one expert that she had Lyme disease. Unfortunately, at that point the disease was already very **advanced**. Amy was treated with antibiotics. However, the lesions on her brain caused her to have **seizures**. Amy knows she must live with her illness for the rest of her life. "I am in this for the long haul," she says. However, she remains hopeful.

Cases of Lyme Disease in the United States

Each yellow dot above represents a case of Lyme disease in 2016. The disease is most common in the Northeast and upper Midwest.

A Tick's Best Friend

Ticks don't just spread disease to humans—they infect pets, too. In April 2015, pet owners Angelo and Diana Scala became worried when they noticed blood flowing from their dog Louie's nose. "The blood wouldn't stop," Diana said. "It was terrifying."

It can be hard to spot a tick in the dense fur of a dog or cat.

A boxer much like the Scalas' dog, Louie

Things only got worse when Louie began throwing up. His back legs also became swollen. The Scalas worried that Louie might not survive. After many trips to the vet, Louie was finally tested for tick-borne diseases. The test came back positive for Rocky Mountain spotted fever. After eighteen days of hospital treatment, Louie was well enough to go home. The Scalas were thrilled to have their best friend back with them.

Pet owners can help keep their pets safe from ticks by applying special medication to their fur.

It's important to wear gloves when removing ticks from dogs. Contact with fluids from infected ticks can spread RMSF to people.

No More Meat

One type of tick—the Lone Star tick—can cause a very strange reaction. After walking her dog in the woods in Maryland, Laura Stirling found a little spotted tick attached to her hip. "I just took it off and threw it away," she said, not thinking it was dangerous.

Laura Stirling

A tiny spotted tick like the one Laura found on her body

Three weeks later, Laura sat down to a meal of pork sausage. Afterward, she became extremely ill. "It was the middle of the night. I woke up covered in **hives**," Laura now recalls. It turned out that the tick bite had caused her to develop an **allergy** to meats, including beef, pork, and lamb, and to dairy products. "I thought it was completely crazy, because I've eaten dairy and red meat all my life," Laura said. Now, because of a single tick, a tiny bite of hamburger can make her sick. "I'm very cautious," she says.

The Lone Star tick gets its name from the white starlike spot on its back.

Each year, over 5,000 people in the United States develop an allergy to meat from a tick bite.

Staying Safe

Problems caused by ticks are only getting worse because of **climate change**. As the weather gets warmer and wetter, there are more places where these bloodsuckers can thrive. "Ticks are being found in new areas where we haven't seen them occurring before," says Benjamin Haynes, a spokesman for the Centers for Disease Control and Prevention (CDC). As a result, people need to take steps to prevent tick bites. For example, it's important to wear long sleeves and pants and to apply insect **repellent** when walking outside.

Many ticks are less active in the winter. If winters become shorter because of climate change, the tick population may grow even larger. Ticks will also have more time to transmit diseases.

Tucking your pants into your socks can help stop ticks from latching on to your legs.

It's also important to check your skin carefully for ticks after you've been outdoors. If you see a tick, remove it with a pair of tweezers and rub the bite with alcohol. Go to a doctor if you develop a rash, fever, or symptoms of any kind. Early **detection** and treatment are the best ways to prevent serious illness. "Don't let a bite change your life," says Benjamin Haynes.

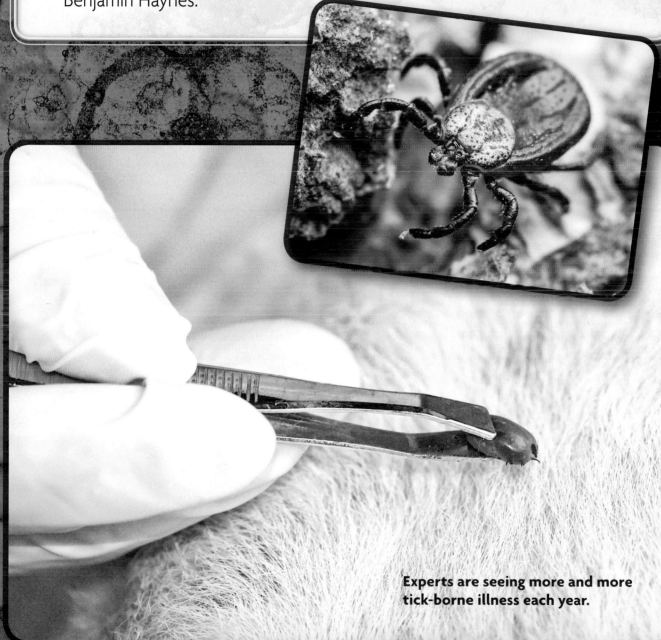

Experts are seeing more and more tick-borne illness each year.

Other Tick-Borne Diseases

In addition to carrying RMSF and Lyme disease, infected ticks can transmit a number of other diseases. Here are some of them:

Babesiosis

Babesiosis (buh-bee-zee-OH-sis) is caused by microscopic parasites and is spread by deer ticks. The disease mostly affects people in the northeastern and midwestern United States. It can cause fever, yellow skin, and dark-colored urine. If untreated, the disease may result in very low blood pressure and even death.

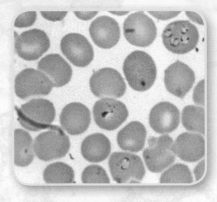
Babesiosis bacteria

A Lone Star tick

Ehrlichiosis

Ehrlichiosis (ur-lik-ee-OH-sis) is a bacterial illness transmitted by Lone Star ticks. Symptoms range from mild body aches to severe fever. If treated quickly, ehrlichiosis generally improves within a few days. If left untreated, some people can experience organ failure and seizures.

Powassan Virus

Powassan (pah-WAH-sen) virus is passed from infected deer ticks to humans. The virus can cause fever, headache, vomiting, confusion, and memory loss. In severe cases, it can lead to brain swelling and death. Most cases occur in the northeastern and upper midwestern United States.

Removing a deer tick from the skin

Glossary

advanced (ad-VANST) fully developed, or moved on to a more serious stage

allergy (AL-er-jee) a physical reaction to something in the environment that's harmless to most people

antibiotics (an-ti-bye-OT-iks) medicines used to destroy or stop the growth of bacteria that cause diseases

arachnids (uh-RAK-nidz) the group of animals that includes scorpions, spiders, and ticks; all arachnids have two main body parts and eight legs

bacteria (bak-TIHR-ee-uh) tiny life-forms that can cause disease

borne (BORN) carried or transported by

climate change (KLYE-mit CHAYNJ) the warming of Earth due to environmental changes, such as a buildup of greenhouse gases that trap the sun's heat

collapsed (kuh-LAPST) fell down and stopped working

detection (di-TEKT-shuhn) the process of finding or locating something

diagnosed (dye-uhg-NOHSD) determined which disease or illness a patient has and what caused it

external parasite (ek-STUR-nuhl PA-ruh-site) an organism that gets food by living on another organism

fatal (FAY-tuhl) deadly

hallucinate (huh-LOO-suh-nate) the experience of seeing things that aren't actually there

hives (HIVES) reddish bumps on the skin

host (HOHST) an animal or plant from which a parasite gets nutrition

insomnia (in-SOM-nee-yah) a condition where a person has difficulty sleeping

lesions (LEE-zhuns) damaged areas of an organ

neurotoxin (NOOR-oh-toks-in) a poison that affects the brain and nervous system

organs (OR-guhnz) parts of the body, such as the lungs, that do a particular job

paralysis (puh-RAL-uh-siss) the inability to move or feel a part of one's body

rare (RAIR) very uncommon

repellent (rih-PEL-uhnt) a chemical used to keep pests away

saliva (suh-LYE-vuh) a clear liquid produced in the mouths of many animals that helps them eat and break down food

seizures (SEE-zhurz) sudden attacks that can cause a person or an animal to shake and lose consciousness

suspected (suh-SPEKT-uhd) something that is believed based on evidence or clues

transmitted (trans-MIT-uhd) passed on from one being to another

transplant (trans-PLANT) an operation in which a diseased organ is replaced by a healthy one

viruses (VYE-ruhss-iz) tiny organisms that can be seen only with powerful microscopes; they can invade cells and cause diseases

Index

Bibliography

Ashley, Jane. "Rocky Mountain spotted fever isn't limited to the Rockies, and it's deadly." *The Washington Post* (November 16, 2015).

Tan, Amy. "My Plight with Lyme Disease." *The New York Times* (August 11, 2013).

Centers for Disease Control and Prevention: www.cdc.gov/ticks/index.html

Read More

Davies, Nicola. *What's Eating You? Parasites—The Inside Story (Animal Science).* Somerville, MA: Candlewick (2009).

Markovics, Joyce L. *Tiny Invaders! Deadly Microorganisms (Nature's Invaders).* North Mankato, MN: Capstone (2014).

Learn More Online

To learn more about ticks, visit
www.bearportpublishing.com/BuggedOut

About the Author

Kevin Blake lives in Providence, Rhode Island, with his wife, Melissa, his son, Sam, and his daughter, Ilana. He has written many nonfiction books for kids.